Living in the Power of the Holy Spirit

A Catholic Bible Study

D0823657

By Rich Cleveland

theWORD
among us®

Emmaus Journey is a discipleship and evangelization ministry that works in and
through Catholic parishes. It was founded by The Navigators,
an interdenominational religious organization.

The Word Among Us Press
9639 Doctor Perry Road
Ijamsville, Maryland 21754
www.wordamongus.org

ISBN: 978-1-59325-035-5

12 11 10 09   8 9 10 11

Cover design by David Crosson

Library of Congress Control Number: 2004109478

Imprimatur: Most Reverend Michael J. Sheridan
Bishop of Colorado Springs
July 8, 2004

The Imprimatur is a declaration that this work does not
contain doctrinal or moral errors.

Acknowledgments

I wish to acknowledge the dedicated help and partnership of Gail Cleveland in the development of these materials. I am also appreciative of the welcoming environment offered by Father Paul Wicker and Holy Apostles Catholic Church. Many individuals freely shared their insights as participants or as leaders of the small groups in which these materials were developed. We are grateful for their help.

Acknowledgments continue on page 101.

Table of Contents

Introduction

Adove. Wind. Fire. These are the images that often come into our minds when we think about the Holy Spirit. While these are all apt images, they don't fully communicate the power that is available to us through the Holy Spirit. How can we as Catholics go beyond these images to encounter the Holy Spirit face to face? How do we cooperate with him to receive the fullness of his presence? How do we receive his fruits and exercise his gifts?

These are a few of the questions explored in this Bible study. As you work through the nine sessions, you will gain a deeper understanding of how the Holy Spirit has worked in the lives of Christians in the past and how he wants to work in your own life today. *Living in the Power of the Holy Spirit* is designed to give you a deeper appreciation for the work of the Spirit in bearing fruit in your life and a greater hunger for his gifts. Transformed by the power of the Holy Spirit, Christians everywhere can more effectively carry on Jesus' mission in the world today.

As you begin, plan on setting aside at least one hour to work through each session. Come with an open heart and mind as you explore the issues raised within these pages. During the course of the Bible study, if the Lord shows you an area in your life that needs changing, be open to change so that the Spirit can work in you and through you.

Living in the Power of the Holy Spirit: A Catholic Bible Study was developed and field-tested through the Small Christian Communities ministry of Holy Apostles Catholic Church in Colorado Springs, Colorado, so it lends itself to use in small groups. However, it can also be used individually or with a spouse or friend. If you are part of a faith-sharing group, plan on spending another hour or two together discussing your journey.

If you are new to a faith-sharing group, here are some helpful attitudes to keep in mind:

1. Preparation. The Bible study discussion is built on the premise that each person has invested the time to think about the passages and answer the questions. To be unprepared turns the Bible study discussions into a sharing of opinions. Though you may not be able to prepare every time, to choose not to prepare deprives the group of the blessings of God working in your life. Selecting a specific time to do your study each week and establishing a consistent place to study can help you be prepared.

In between sessions, it is highly recommended that you keep a prayer journal. While praying each day and reading Scripture, you may have thoughts that are inspired by the Lord. If he is speaking a word to you, you may want to share what he's told you with the group. A prayer journal will help you to remember whatever it is you have learned through your daily Scripture reading and prayer.

2. Teachability. Try to be open to discover new truths and look at old truths in a new way. We always learn when we are open to new concepts.

3. Wholeheartedness. There may be days when you feel too depleted emotionally and spiritually to participate in the Bible discussion. While it is helpful to acknowledge these feelings, giving in to them can negatively affect the whole group's experience. God can use the discussion and community experiences to lift your spirits. Try to participate enthusiastically even when you don't feel like it.

4. Willingness to Apply What You've Learned. The purpose of a Bible study is to change lives, which means changing our attitudes and behavior. The process of bringing new attitudes and behaviors to life is stifled when we close ourselves off to the attitudes and behavior changes we feel

God is asking of us. On the other hand, when we apply the truths we've discovered in the Scriptures, our lives can change dramatically. These will grow into mature values as we continue to follow Christ.

5. Respect for All Contributions and Contributors to the Discussion. Each of the members of your group will approach the study from different backgrounds and different ways of thinking. Each person has a valuable contribution to make. It is important to listen and learn from one another.

A special guide is available for leaders of small groups. It includes suggestions for handling the various sessions and for creating and sustaining positive small-group dynamics. This guide can be downloaded for free at www.emmausjourney.org.

Finally, it is my prayer that through this Bible study, the Holy Spirit will enkindle your heart and set it ablaze with love for God.

Rich Cleveland

Session 1

Meditating on God's Word

▶ Before You Begin

Get acquainted with the others in your group by sharing your answers to these questions:
- What is your name?
- What's the best gift you have ever received? Why?

> An Oriental fable tells of three horsemen who were traveling through the desert at night. Unexpectedly they were confronted by a mysterious person. The stranger told them that they would soon cross the dry bed of a stream.
>
> "When you arrive there," he declared, "get off your horses and fill your pockets and saddle bags from the river bed. At sunrise examine the stones you have picked up. You will be both glad and sorry."
>
> As the man predicted, the travelers came to a dry stream bed. In a spirit of adventure they put a few of the many stones they found scattered about into their pockets. At sunrise the next day they examined the pebbles they had picked up. To their great astonishment they found the stones had been transformed into diamonds, rubies, emeralds and other precious stones.
>
> Recalling the statement of the stranger in the desert, they understood what he meant—they were glad for the pebbles they had picked up but sorry they hadn't taken more.
>
> —Jim Downing, *Meditation: The Bible Tells You How*

In a similar way, this small-group community experience can be likened to the stream in this fable. Each week as you invest some time studying Scripture and praying, you dismount from the busyness of your travels through life long enough to pick up some precious spiritual stones. And as you meet each week to share these nuggets of truth and pearls of spiritual wisdom, you will discover that, in Christ, you are enriched.

Meditating on the truths of Scripture transforms ordinary observations into spiritual treasure. Jim Downing, a Christian evangelist who wrote *Meditation: The Bible Tells You How*, likens meditation to rumination:

Many animals, among which are cattle, sheep, goats, antelope, camels, and giraffes, are in a class called ruminant animals. They have four stomachs each, or to be more technical, each has a stomach with four compartments. The first part or the first stomach is called the rumen. The way this particular class of animal goes about the digestive process is not the most elegant by human standards. If you've ever watched a dairy cow eat bluegrass, you will notice that she goes out early in the morning, puts her head down like a mowing machine, and never lifts it until someone disturbs her. She really concentrates on eating. . . .

Then about ten o'clock in the morning, when the sun begins to get hot, the animal lies down in the shade and regurgitates the food out of stomach one, the rumen. This time it chews it thoroughly. The food then goes into stomachs two, three, and four. Eventually the digested food is absorbed into the animal's blood stream, and literally becomes part of its life.

Meditation is like rumination in that once you have gleaned an idea from Scripture, you pray and think about it, discuss it, and go back and think about it some more. The more you chew on God's word, the more nourishment enters your spiritual blood stream, bringing strength, transformation, and renewal.

As you begin this nine-week experience, try to dismount from the busy-ness of your life and load your pockets with many spiritual stones. Allow God to transform these stones into spiritual treasures, which will enrich your life. We hope that you will develop the habit of meditating (or chewing) on God's word, both individually and as a community, and thereby receive much spiritual nourishment.

Meditation Exercise

You can meditate on Scripture in a number of practical ways. In this session we will experiment with several different techniques of meditating on Scripture.

Method A: The first method involves restating a passage in your own words. Think about synonymous words and phrases to capture the meaning of the passage. In the example below, Joshua 1:8 is broken down into phrases. In the space provided, state each phrase in your own words.

This book of the law   _____

shall not depart out of your mouth;   _____

you shall meditate on it day and night,   _____

so that you may be careful   _____

to act in accordance   _____

with all that is written in it.   _____

For then you shall make your way

prosperous,   _____

and then you shall be successful.   _____

Method B: A second method of enhancing scriptural meditation is to ask a series of questions about a passage that will require you to think more deeply about its meaning. These questions help bring new insight to a portion of Scripture. Below are two examples of the kind of questions you can use:

Question Method 1
Who: Who are the people involved?
What: What is the incident or issue?
When: When do these things happen?
Where: Describe the environment?
Why: What is the reasoning?
How: What is the process?

Question Method 2
Is there a behavior or attitude to avoid?
Is there a promise I should rely on?
Is there an example for me to follow?
Is there an instruction to obey?
Is there new information about God the Father, Jesus, or the Holy Spirit?

Using one or both of these methods, think through Psalm 1:1-3 below, and record your questions and thoughts in the space provided.

Happy are those
    who do not follow the advice of the wicked,
or take the path that sinners tread,
    or sit in the seat of scoffers;
but their delight is in the law of the LORD,
    and on his law they meditate day and night.
They are like trees
    planted by streams of water,
which yield their fruit in its season,

and their leaves do not wither.
In all that they do, they prosper.

_____

_____

_____

_____

Method C: Another helpful method is to reflect on a passage of Scripture and then pray through it. Praying through a passage helps you reflect on your life and the lives of those you know. Then you can talk to God about your life in relation to the truths in the passage. In this session you have meditated on two wonderful passages. Take the next few minutes and pray about the truths of Psalm 1:1-3 and Joshua 1:8. Record your thoughts in the space below.

_____

_____

_____

_____

_____

 Preparing for Session 2

1. Each day, read some Scripture, perhaps meditating on one of the passages above that has touched you. Don't forget to record your thoughts in your prayer journal.

2. Complete the questions for the next session, "Who Is the Holy Spirit and How Does He Work?"

Notes for Session 1

Notes for Session 1

Session 2

Who Is the Holy Spirit and How Does He Work?

▶ Before You Begin

Take a few minutes to share insights with the other members in your Bible study from your prayer time and daily Scripture reading.

We believe in the Holy Spirit, the Lord, the giver of life,
who proceeds from the Father and the Son,
with the Father and Son he is worshipped and glorified.
He has spoken through the Prophets.

Each Sunday during Mass, when we recite the Nicene Creed, we affirm our belief in the Holy Spirit. Yet, how many of us have a conscious awareness and dependence on the Holy Spirit's activity in our life, in the world, or in history? Here are a few questions we'll consider as we begin this study:

▶ **How did the Holy Spirit work in people's lives in the early church?**
▶ **How can we understand and experience the many aspects of the Spirit through the names and symbols used to describe him?**
▶ **What is the Holy Spirit's role as the third Person of the Trinity?**
▶ **How does the Spirit want to work in your life in the coming weeks?**

At the beginning of Jesus' public ministry, John the Baptist said that while he was baptizing with water for repentance, someone greater than he would come to baptize "with the Holy Spirit and fire" (Matthew 3:11). Later, near the end of his ministry, Jesus told the apostles that it was to their advantage that he leave and return to his Father, "for if I do not go away, the Advocate [the Holy Spirit] will not come to you" (John 16:7). The implication of these two statements to Jesus' ministry is that the *Holy Spirit is essential to our lives as believers.* Consequently, we must do whatever we can to come to know the Holy Spirit more deeply so that we can confidently yield ourselves to his influence and guidance in our lives.

The Holy Spirit's Actions in People's Lives

1. (a) Many times in Scripture, the Holy Spirit has made his presence known by being uniquely involved in the lives of people. Review the following passages and determine what the Holy Spirit was doing and which biblical character was being affected.

Reference	Whose Life Was Touched?	What Is the Spirit's Action?
Genesis 1:26-27 and Psalm 104:30		
Luke 1:30-35		
Luke 1:39-45		
John 1:30-34		
Romans 8:10-11		
Acts 2:1-4, 16-21		
Acts 13:2		

(b) What is your initial impression of the Holy Spirit based on these occurrences?

_____

_____

_____

_____

The Many Biblical Names of the Holy Spirit

In many cultures a person is given a name that characterizes some trait or feature about that person. In the New Testament, the Holy Spirit has also been given various descriptive names and titles. These include: Advocate or Counselor (John 14:16); the Spirit of truth (John 16:13); the Spirit of the promise (Galatians 3:14); the Spirit of God (Romans 8:9); the Spirit of Christ (1 Peter 1:11); the Spirit of life (Romans 8:2); the Spirit of grace (Hebrews 10:29); and the Spirit of adoption (Romans 8:15). In addition, various terms and symbols have been used to symbolize his presence, including: fire (Acts 2:3-4); a dove (Matthew 3:16); water (John 7:38-39); wind (Acts 2:2); a seal (John 6:27); and a cloud (Luke 9:34-35).

2. (a) Choose three descriptive terms or symbols of the Holy Spirit and read the accompanying Scripture reference. Why is the Spirit described with that particular name?

    _____

    _____

    _____

    _____

    (b) In what ways would you like to more deeply experience the Holy Spirit in the coming weeks? (For example, you might want to experience the Spirit as fire so that you have a more burning love and desire for the Lord.)

    _____

    _____

    _____

    _____

The Role of the Third Person of the Trinity

3. (a) In Ephesians 1:3-14, St. Paul describes how the three Persons of the Trinity cooperate to invite us to share in God's life and become his children. As you read the passage, identify and describe the role of the Father (verses 3-6), the Son (verses 7-12), and the Holy Spirit (verses 13-14) in God's plan of salvation.

    _____

    _____

    _____

(b) Identify and describe the ways in which you can see the Father working in the world today.

_____

_____

_____

_____

(c) What impact has Jesus' work of redemption had on your life personally?

_____

_____

_____

_____

(d) Think of one example in which the Spirit's work in one person (perhaps a saint) had an enormous impact on his or her world.

_____

_____

_____

> Inseparable in what they are, the divine persons are also inseparable in what they do. But within the single divine operation each shows forth what is proper to him in the Trinity, especially in the divine missions of the Son's Incarnation and the gift of the Holy Spirit.
> —*Catechism of the Catholic Church, 267*

4. (a) According to the following passages, how does the Holy Spirit work in us to increase our faith?

1 Corinthians 2:9-16:

_____

_____

_____

_____

1 Corinthians 12:1-3:

_____

_____

_____

_____

Galatians 4:4-7:

_____

_____

_____

_____

(b) What are some of the benefits of the Holy Spirit dwelling within us, according to Romans 8:9-11, 16-17?

_____

_____

_____

_____

How Can We Respond to the Holy Spirit?

5. Although we rely completely on the Spirit's grace and work in our lives, our daily cooperation is a vital component in our walk with the Lord. Reflect on the following verses and identify what our initial response to the Holy Spirit should entail.

Ephesians 1:13-14:

_____

_____

_____

_____

Galatians 3:1-5, 13-14:

_____

_____

_____

_____

1 Peter 1:2:

_____

_____

_____

_____

Obedience to Jesus Christ is the hallmark of conversion through the Holy Spirit. For many of the first Christians, it began with their initial obedience to believe and be baptized, or in the case with many of us who were born into Catholic families, to be baptized as infants and believe more fully as we mature in our faith. God intends that this initial obedience of putting our trust and faith in Jesus Christ grow in depth and responsiveness to Jesus as we yield to the continuing sanctifying grace of the Holy Spirit.

6. As Catholics, we are encouraged to affirm our initial steps of faith by continuing to live a life guided by the Holy Spirit. According to the Gospel of Luke, Simeon was a man on whom the Holy Spirit "rested." Read Luke 2:25-35 and then answer the following questions.

(a) How is Simeon described in verse 25? What do you think was the relationship between the kind of life he led and the Holy Spirit's presence in him?

_____

_____

_____

_____

(b) What had the Holy Spirit revealed to Simeon? What kind of inner disposition do you think Simeon had to have in order to hear the Holy Spirit and be guided by him?

_____

_____

_____

_____

(c) According to this passage, what results can we expect when we live life in the Spirit?

_____

_____

_____

_____

(d) What are some practical ways we can learn to be guided by the Holy Spirit?

_____

_____

_____

_____

7. As we come to the end of this session, share one new truth you have learned so far about the Holy Spirit and his desire to touch and influence your life.

_____

_____

_____

_____

Pray Together:

Come, Creator Spirit,
visit the minds of those who are yours;
fill with heavenly grace
the hearts that you have made.

Grant we may know the Father through you,
and come to know the Son as well,
and may we always cling in faith
to you, the Spirit of them both.

(Stanzas 1 and 6 from *Veni Creator*, appearing in
Come, Creator Spirit by Raniero Cantalamessa)

▶ Preparing for Session 3

1. Each day, read some Scripture, perhaps meditating on one of the passages above that has touched you. Don't forget to record your thoughts in your prayer journal.

2. Complete the questions for the next session, "The Holy Spirit, God's Greatest Gift to Us."

Notes for Session 2

Session 3

The Holy Spirit, God's Greatest Gift to Us

▶ Before You Begin

Take a few minutes to share insights with the other members in your Bible study from your prayer time and daily Scripture reading.

During his second Christmas, our first grandchild was overwhelmed by the abundance of the presents he received from parents, grandparents, aunts, and uncles. The enthusiasm of the adults as they watched him open his first few gifts, and the noise and confusion around him, were just too much. He began to cry, and then shied away from opening more presents. His mom and dad wisely set aside the rest of his gifts so that he could open them on another day.

As baptized Christians, we too have been given an abundance of gifts, but sometimes we fail—at least initially—to appreciate them. During Jesus' last evening with the apostles, he introduced three gifts that would, despite his impending absence, make his presence known on earth for all time. In their last fleeting hours together, Jesus gave his followers his everlasting presence in the Eucharist (Matthew 26:26-30), in his word (John 14:23-24), and in his Spirit (John 14:15-17). All three make it possible for us to experience the fullness of life in him.

Unlike our grandson's response to his gifts, we may sometimes be "under-whelmed" by these gifts of love and life that have been made available to us. Like our grandson's presents left under the tree, we may set aside God's gifts—untouched, unwrapped, and therefore unavailable. This session encourages us to unwrap a fuller understanding of one of these gifts—the Holy Spirit—as we explore the following questions:

New Life in the Spirit

The more we meditate on and begin to comprehend the Spirit, the more we will want to experience his power and presence in our lives. As Pope John Paul II has noted: "The 'good news' is directed to stirring a person to a conversion of heart and life and a clinging to Jesus Christ as Lord and Savior; to disposing a person to receive Baptism and the Eucharist and to strengthen a person in the prospect and realization of *new life according to the Spirit*" (*Christifideles Laici*, 33; emphasis added).

It is important that we not view these passages on the gift of the Holy Spirit and this "new life according to the Spirit" solely as individuals. The Holy Spirit was given collectively to the body of Christ, the church. Although we each need personal knowledge and experience of the Spirit's work in our lives, we become partakers of the Holy Spirit and the promises associated with him as a member of his body. Consequently, as you consider these passages you should do so in light of the implications they have both for you personally and for other members of the People of God.

The Holy Spirit Is God's Gift to Us

1. (a) How would you define a "gift"? What makes the Holy Spirit a
   gift?

   _____

   _____

   _____

   _____

(b) In light of John 14:16 and 15:26, who sent the Holy Spirit?

_____

_____

_____

_____

> The eternal origin of the Holy Spirit is revealed in his mission in time. The Spirit is sent to the apostles and to the Church both by the Father in the name of the Son, and by the Son in person once he had returned to the Father. The sending of the person of the Spirit after Jesus' glorification reveals in its fullness the mystery of the Holy Trinity.
>
> —*Catechism of the Catholic Church,* 244

The Spirit Draws Us Close to the Father and the Son

2. (a) In John 14:15-29, 15:26, and 16:4-15, Jesus explains how the gift of the Spirit can draw us closer to God. After reflecting on these passages, list three or more reasons why Jesus gave us his Spirit.

_____

_____

_____

_____

(b) According to the same passages, what purposes would be fulfilled by the coming of the Spirit?

_____

_____

_____

_____

(c) How are these purposes being fulfilled in the church today?

_____

_____

_____

_____

The Spirit Works in Us to Build the Church

3. Many New Testament passages testify to the work of the Holy Spirit in the life of the early church. Look up the following passages, and briefly describe what the Holy Spirit does for us.

Acts 1:8:

_____

_____

1 Corinthians 2:12-13:

_____

_____

Ephesians 3:16:

_____

_____

1 Thessalonians 1:6:

_____

_____

4. The Acts of the Apostles has been called the "gospel of the Holy Spirit," because it shows how vibrant the church is when the Spirit is at work. Without the action of the Holy Spirit, the early church—and the church today—could not grow, because the Holy Spirit is the power and the love of God that touches people

and builds the body of Christ. Based on the following passages, how did the Holy Spirit help the early church to grow?

Acts 2:1-13, 41:

_____

_____

_____

_____

Acts 8:26-40:

_____

_____

_____

_____

Acts 10:19-48:

_____

_____

_____

_____

5. Of the roles and actions of the Holy Spirit identified so far, which are the two that you would most like to see him accomplish in your life? Why?

_____

_____

_____

_____

Obstacles to Receiving the Spirit

6. (a) According to the following passages, what can prevent us from receiving all that the Holy Spirit has for us and desires to do in and through us?

Ephesians 4:30-32:

_____

_____

_____

_____

Romans 8:5-9:

_____

_____

_____

_____

1 Thessalonians 5:19-22:

_____

_____

_____

_____

(b) What are some practical things we can do to ensure that our mind is set on the things of the Spirit and not on the things of the flesh?

_____

_____

_____

_____

7. According to the following passages, what can we do if we feel that we may have suppressed the Spirit's actions in our life in the past?

1 John 1:9:

_____

_____

_____

_____

Romans 8:26-27:

_____

_____

_____

_____

8. Describe how the Holy Spirit is a special gift from God to you.

_____

_____

_____

_____

Pray Together:

You are named the Paraclete,
gift of God most high,
living fountain, fire, love
and anointing for the soul.

Grant we may know the Father through you,
and come to know the Son as well,
and may we always cling in faith
to you, the Spirit of them both.

(Stanzas 2 and 6 from *Veni Creator*, appearing in
Come, Creator Spirit by Raniero Cantalamessa)

▶ Preparing for Session 4

1. Each day, read some Scripture, perhaps meditating on one of the passages above that has touched you. Don't forget to record your thoughts in your prayer journal.

2. Complete the questions for the next session, "The Work of the Spirit . . . to Bear Fruit for God."

Notes for Session 3

Session 4

The Work of the Spirit . . . to Bear Fruit for God

Take a few minutes to share insights with the other members in your Bible study from your prayer time and daily Scripture reading.

When Jesus promised that he came so that we might "have life, and have it abundantly" (John 10:10), he was not speaking simply of living eternally after death. He also was holding forth the promise that we could experience new life—that is, a new quality of life—here and now. Today, God's children can be set free from the enslaving habits of the flesh. God has promised that our lives should be and can be marked by new qualities and characteristics—the result of the supernatural, indwelling, and distinctive work of the Holy Spirit. This session focuses on the Holy Spirit's work in us, the fruit of which is the transformation and reshaping of our character. We will explore the following questions:

▶ How can we learn from the Holy Spirit to abide in Christ so that we bear fruit in our lives?

▶ What affects our ability to stay close to God and bear spiritual fruit?

▶ In what areas of our lives are we damaging our relationship with God and therefore failing to bear fruit?

The Fruits of the Spirit Are Available to All of Us

Webster's New World Dictionary defines the word "character" as a distinctive work, trait, quality, or attribute, or an individual's pattern of behavior or personality. We may all possess different gifts, but the fruits of the Holy Spirit, expressed as Christian character, are available to all of us. In fact, they should be present in all who abide in Christ. As Pope John Paul II explains:

Engrafted to the vine and brought to life, the branches are expected to bear fruit. . . . Bearing fruit is an essential demand of life in Christ and life in the Church. The person who does not bear fruit does not remain in communion: "Each branch of mine that bears no fruit, he (my Father) takes away" (John 15:2).

Communion with Jesus, which gives rise to the communion of Christians among themselves, is an indispensable condition for bearing fruit: "Apart from me you can do nothing" (John 15:5). And communion with others is the most magnificent fruit that the branches can give: in fact, it is the gift of Christ and His Spirit.

—*Christifideles Laici*, 32

Fruit is that part of a flowering plant that contains the seeds. The word "fruit" comes from the Latin word *frui*, which means "enjoy." When these fruitful qualities and characteristics of the Spirit are in your life, not only do you enjoy life more fully but others more fully enjoy you. Often it is these "Christ in you" qualities that become the seeds of evangelization, springing up as new life in others. Perhaps this is what Jesus meant when he said, "Let your light shine before others, so that they may see your good works and give glory to your Father in heaven" (Matthew 5:16).

Abiding in Christ: The Key to Bearing Fruit

1. (a) In the first book of the Bible, God instructed Adam and Eve to "be fruitful and multiply" (Genesis 1:28). Beginning with this creation account and continuing throughout the Old and New Testaments, the theme of bearing fruit appears frequently. The prophet Jeremiah used such an analogy to describe two kinds of people and the inevitable consequences they experience as a result of their choices. Take a look at this analogy in Jeremiah 17:5-14. What images does Jeremiah use to describe these two types of people?

_____

_____

_____

_____

(b) According to Jeremiah, what is the key attribute of the person who bears fruit?

_____

_____

_____

_____

(c) What do the terms "trust in the Lord" and "trust in man" mean to you?

_____

_____

_____

_____

2. (a) In the New Testament, the Gospel of John continues to speak about the importance of bearing fruit and the process of becoming fruitful. Read and reflect on Jesus' statements in John 15:1-16. What do you think Jesus meant by bearing fruit?

_____

_____

_____

_____

(b) Which of Jesus' statements most motivates you to live your life in a way that bears fruit? Why?

_____

_____

_____

_____

(c) Since abiding in Christ is the key to bearing fruit in our lives, practically speaking, what does "abide in Christ" mean to you?

_____

_____

_____

_____

What Affects Our Ability to Bear Fruit?

3. In Galatians 5:16-25, St. Paul wrote about some of the factors that affect our ability to stay close to God and bear spiritual fruit. Desires within us cause a battle to rage between "the spirit" and "the flesh."

(a) What do you think St. Paul meant when he used the word "flesh"? How does this differ from our physical bodies, which are created by God and therefore are good?

_____

_____

_____

_____

(b) What does this passage teach about the influence of the flesh?

_____

_____

_____

_____

(c) What do these verses tell you about the Holy Spirit's influence?

_____

_____

_____

_____

(d) Explain the difference between living by the flesh and living by the Spirit.

_____

_____

_____

_____

4. In John 12:23-26, Jesus refers to his impending sacrifice on the cross and explains what conditions are necessary to bear fruit in our lives. What truths do you find mentioned here? Describe and explain your emotional response to them.

_____

_____

_____

_____

Facing Those Areas That Prevent Us from Bearing Fruit

5. If we belong to Jesus Christ, according to St. Paul, we have crucified the flesh with its passions and desires (Galatians 5:24). Use the following list, found in Galatians 5:19-23, to evaluate whether these works of the flesh are present in any way in your life. Do this evaluation in private, and then discuss whatever you feel comfortable sharing with your group. Make the same evaluation for the fruits of the Spirit. Indicate whether each characteristic is:

(1) frequently present   (2) occasionally present

(3) seldom present   (4) never present

The Works of the Flesh

__fornication

__impurity

__licentiousness [unrestrained by law or morality]

__idolatry

__sorcery [witchcraft; in the ancient world, the use of drugs] ___enmities [hatred, hostility]

___strife [bitter conflict or rivalry]

___jealousy

___anger [uncontrolled bursts of temper]

___quarrels

___dissensions [partisan or contentious divisions]

___factions [contentious minority within a larger group]

___envy

___drunkenness

___carousing [drunken revelry]

The Fruits of the Spirit*

___love

___joy

___peace

___patience [long-suffering]

___kindness

___goodness

___faithfulness

___gentleness [meekness]

___self-control [temperance]

___modesty

___chastity

___generosity

* The tradition of the Catholic Church lists twelve fruits of the Spirit (*Catechism of the Catholic Church*, 1832). However, we will confine our reflections in future sessions to the first nine characteristics above which are listed in Galatians 5:22-23.

Take some time in private reflection to be honest with God about what you see in your life. Where necessary, confess your failure to allow the Spirit's fruit to abide in you. In every area where you see sin patterns, repent and turn away from these sins. Take advantage of the Sacrament of Reconciliation, knowing that in Jesus' blood, all your sins are forgiven. Then accept the forgiveness that is assured you through Jesus Christ. Acknowledge the fruit you've seen the Holy Spirit work in you, and give thanks and praise to him. Write a brief prayer asking God to help you yield to the Holy Spirit's influence in your life rather than to the flesh.

> "No good tree bears bad fruit, nor again does a bad tree bear good fruit; for each tree is known by its own fruit. Figs are not gathered from thorns, nor are grapes picked from a bramble bush."
>
> —*Luke 6:43-44*

6. Jesus talks about storing up treasures in our heart that will produce good actions and attitudes. What are some practical ways we can store good things in our hearts?

    _____

    _____

    _____

    _____

7. What basic truths about bearing fruit did you discover in this session?

    _____

    _____

    _____

    _____

When we consciously decide to turn away from the works of the flesh, we can choose to live according to the Spirit. Over the next few weeks, we will look at some specific ways that the Spirit wants to form our character so that we more clearly reflect Jesus' image in the world around us. The next four sessions will enable us to delve more deeply into each of the fruits of the Holy Spirit listed in Galatians 5:22-23.

Pray Together:

Kindle a light in our senses,
pour love into our hearts,
infirmities of this body of ours
overcoming with strength secure.

Grant we may know the Father through you,
and come to know the Son as well,
and may we always cling in faith
to you, the Spirit of them both.

(Stanzas 4 and 6 from *Veni Creator,* appearing in
Come, Creator Spirit by Raniero Cantalamessa)

▶ Preparing for Session 5

1. Each day, read some Scripture, perhaps meditating on one of the passages above that has touched you. Don't forget to record your thoughts in your prayer journal.

2. Complete the questions for the next session, "The Fruits of the Spirit Are Love and Joy."

Notes for Session 4

Session 5

The Fruits of the Spirit Are Love and Joy

Take a few minutes to share insights with the other members in your Bible study from your prayer time and daily Scripture reading.

In this session we will look at two characteristics of the Holy Spirit's fruit: love and joy. These qualities may be the wellspring from which flow all the other spiritual fruits. We will explore the following questions:

► How did Jesus express his love for others?
► How is the fruit of love active in my life, and where does it need to grow?
► What gives us a deep and lasting joy?
► How do we claim God's promise so that the fruit of joy can sustain us even in difficult times?

The Fruit of the Spirit Is Love

> Perhaps we do not know what love is: it would not surprise me a great deal to learn this, for love consists, not in the extent of our happiness, but in the firmness of our determination to try to please God in everything.
> —**St. Teresa of Avila**, *Interior Castle*

Many of us would have to agree with St. Teresa of Avila! Often our concept of love comes from people we've known—parents, relatives, and friends who have both experienced and manifested an inadequate understanding of love. To break this chain of misunderstanding, we must come to know and encounter real love, God's love. Then we must become contagious carriers of real love to real people—those whom we encounter each day.

Jesus, sent by the Father, revealed to us how much God loves us and showed us perfectly how to love others. Through meditation on Jesus' life and teachings and through communion with him, we allow ourselves to be loved by him. When we allow our minds and hearts to be transformed by his love, our anger, hurts, fear, and feelings of unworthiness will be dissolved in his unconditional love. We will then find ourselves becoming bearers of God's love to those around us.

> **The Greek Translation**
>
> *Agape*, the Christian word [for love], means unconquerable benevolence. . . . It is a feeling of the mind as much as of the heart; it concerns the will as much as the emotions. It describes the deliberate effort—which we can make only with the help of God—never to seek anything but the best, even for those who seek the worst for us.
> —**William Barclay**, *The Daily Bible Study Series*

Love is the primary fruit of the Holy Spirit and is therefore held up throughout the New Testament as our highest goal as Christians. St. John wrote that "God is love" (1 John 4:8), and St. Paul called love the greatest of the Christian virtues (1 Corinthians 13:13).

Jesus' Example of Love

Each year during Holy Week, Christians commemorate the Last Supper, when Jesus washed his apostles' feet and gave them his body and blood. Jesus' words to his followers that evening about love are even more poignant when we realize that he also washed the feet of Judas, his betrayer.

1. (a) Read John 13:1-17, 34-35. Imagine that you are one of the apostles that evening, perhaps Peter, James, or John. How do you think you would feel about Jesus' expression of love?

    _____

    _____

    _____

    _____

(b) In your own words, how do you understand the message of John 13:34-35? How does our experience of Jesus' love empower us to love others?

_____

_____

_____

_____

2 (a) Based on 1 John 4:7-19, why do we know that God loves us?

_____

_____

_____

_____

(b) What connection is made in this passage between our love for God and our love for our brothers and sisters?

_____

_____

_____

_____

Without love, the outward work is of no value; but whatever is done out of love, be it never so little, is wholly fruitful. For God regards the greatness of the love that prompts a man, rather than the greatness of his achievement.

—**Thomas à Kempis**, *The Imitation of Christ*

How Am I Bearing the Fruit of Love?

3. In 1 Corinthians 13:4-7, Paul describes love's actions in both
   positive and negative ways:

Love is *patient.*	Love is *not envious.*
Love is *kind.*	Love is *not boastful.*
Love *rejoices with the truth*	Love is *not arrogant.*
Love *bears all things,*	Love is *not rude.*
believes all things,	Love does *not insist on its own way.*
hopes all things,	Love is *not irritable.*
endures all things.	Love is *not resentful.*
	Love does *not rejoice over wrongdoing.*

Think of specific instances over the past few weeks when you found
it challenging to be loving to someone in the ways described by St. Paul.
How can you better express your love in the future?

_____

_____

_____

_____

The great message that we have to carry, as ministers
of God's word and followers of Jesus, is that God loves
us not because of what we do or accomplish, but
because God has created and redeemed us in love and
has chosen us to proclaim that love as the true source
of all human life.

—Henri J. M. Nouwen, *In the Name of Jesus:
Reflections on Christian Leadership*

The Fruit of the Spirit Is Joy

When we are experiencing real love, it produces real joy in us. Blessed Mother Teresa, who gave her life to serving the poorest of the poor, and herself lived a life of poverty, discovered that, "Joy is prayer, joy is strength, joy is love, joy is a net of love by which you can catch souls." Mother Teresa bore this fruit of the Spirit by radiating her joy in the Lord to others.

> **The Greek Translation**
>
> The Greek [for joy] is *chara*, and the characteristic of this word is that it most often describes that joy which has a basis in religion. . . . It is not the joy that comes from earthly things, still less from triumphing over someone else in competition. It is a joy whose foundation is God.
> —**William Barclay**, *The Daily Bible Study Series*

All Christians can radiate joy. Repeatedly St. Paul admonished the community of believers to "rejoice in the Lord always" (Philippians 4:4; see also 1 Thessalonians 5:16 and 2 Corinthians 13:9). These words imply that some New Testament believers needed to be reminded to avoid a long-faced, gloomy disposition and pursue glad-hearted, exuberant living. For St. Paul, joyous living was not only possible but expected, because Jesus had truly transformed their lives.

When people pursue mere pleasure instead of true joy, they are climbing a ladder that's leaning against the wrong wall. Scripture tells us that Jesus endured the pain and sadness of crucifixion "for the sake of the joy that was set before him" (Hebrews 12:2). If real joy could provide such strength and motivation for Jesus, is it not critical that Christians discover and pursue the way of joy themselves?

What Gives Us a Deep and Lasting Joy?

4. Joy seems to be present in the lives of those who are able to view earthly realities in the light of a heavenly perspective. The following passages reveal several factors that can give us a deep and lasting joy. Read each passage and then answer the question:

Psalm 9:1-2: Why does recounting to others how God has worked bring us genuine joy?

_____

_____

_____

_____

Luke 10:17-20: Why is it important to know where our names are written?

_____

_____

_____

_____

Luke 15:4-10: Why do you think Jesus links repentance with joy?

_____

_____

_____

_____

Philippians 1:12-18: How does doing God's will, in this case by preaching the gospel, bring us joy?

_____

_____

_____

_____

1 Thessalonians 1:4-6: Who is the source of our joy?

_____

_____

_____

_____

Joy Even in Suffering

Claiming God's promises when we are suffering is the best way to find the joy of the Spirit. In the midst of turmoil, we can hold on to the truth that God is forming us as his disciples through suffering, and that he disciplines us because he loves us (Hebrews 12:6). We can be confident of our eternal inheritance in heaven and acknowledge that Jesus suffered as well, and that we are not alone.

5. The writers of the New Testament often link joy to persecution and trials. According to the following passages, how can we maintain a spirit of joy during difficult times?

    James 1:2-4:

    _____

    _____

    _____

    _____

    1 Peter 1:6-9:

    _____

    _____

    _____

    _____

1 Peter 4:12-14:

_____

_____

_____

_____

The great hymn writer Fanny Crosby, who lost her sight when she was just six weeks old, demonstrates what it means to maintain an eternal perspective in the midst of difficult current realities:

> Oh, what a happy soul am I,
> Although I cannot see
> I am resolved that in this world
> Contented I will be.
>
> How many blessings I enjoy
> That other people don't!
> To weep and sigh because I'm blind
> I cannot nor I won't.

6. You have discovered many reasons to be a joyful believer, yet you may still find yourself getting spiritually down, even depressed. According to the following passages, what did the psalmists do to recapture and maintain joy?

Psalm 16:8-9, 11:

_____

_____

_____

_____

Psalm 28:7:

_____

_____

_____

_____

Psalm 51:8-13:

_____

_____

_____

_____

> May the God of hope fill you with all joy and peace in believing, so that you may abound in hope by the power of the Holy Spirit.
>
> —*Romans 15:13*

Pray Together:

The enemy drive from us away,
peace then give without delay;
with you as guide to lead the way
we avoid all cause of harm.

Grant we may know the Father through you,
and come to know the Son as well,
and may we always cling in faith
to you, the Spirit of them both.

(Stanzas 5 and 6 from *Veni Creator,* appearing in *Come, Creator Spirit* by Raniero Cantalamessa)

▶ Preparing for Session 6

1. Each day, read some Scripture, perhaps meditating on one of the passages above that has touched you. Don't forget to record your thoughts in your prayer journal.

2. Complete the questions for the next session, "The Fruits of the Spirit Are Peace and Patience."

Notes for Session 5

Session 6

The Fruits of the Spirit Are Peace and Patience

Take a few minutes to share insights with the other members in your Bible study from your prayer time and daily Scripture reading.

Much of the turmoil in this world, whether interpersonal or among political, ethnic, or religious groups, is because we don't treat one another as Christ has treated us. In this session we will reflect on peace and patience (also called long-suffering). Peace and long-suffering are two sides of the same coin. When we dwell in peace we are able to extend the peace of the Spirit to others in the form of long-suffering. In this session, we'll explore the following questions:

▶ Why is God our only source of real and lasting peace?

▶ Where in our lives do we lack peace, whether in our own hearts and minds, in our relationship with God, or in our relationships with others?

▶ How has our Father shown his patience and long-suffering with his people and with us?

▶ How can exercising the gift of patience make us more like Jesus?

The Fruit of the Spirit Is Peace

Peace needn't be elusive; it is a gift Jesus bequeaths to us. "Peace I leave with you; my peace I give to you" (John 14:27). Peace is a gift that resides in Jesus and comes to us through the Holy Spirit as we learn to trust the Father as Jesus did. Peace requires that we hear the message of the risen Lord, "Do not be afraid" (Matthew 28:10), with the inner ear of our heart.

Christians are participants with Christ in spreading the good news that peace has been restored between God and man through him. Whenever we as Jesus' disciples withhold peace through anger, unforgiveness, or simple dislike, we subtly ignore the Spirit who dwells in us and refuse to listen to his voice in our hearts. If not resolved fairly quickly, we soon find ourselves distant from God, and we may feel tension in other relationships as well. That is why it is so essential that you allow the Holy Spirit to produce his fruit in you, including the gift of peace.

The Greek Translation

Usually in the New Testament *eirene* [peace] stands for the Hebrew *shalom* and means not just freedom from trouble but everything that makes for a man's highest good. Here it means that tranquility of heart which derives from the all-pervading consciousness that our times are in the hands of God.

—**William Barclay**, *The Daily Bible Study Series*

As Elizabeth Seton wrote, "From Him [peace] proceeds, to Him it tends, and in Him concentrates." As you prepare the materials for this session, be attentive to your inner spirit. Ask yourself, "Am I at peace?" Ask the Holy Spirit to enable you to discover the sources of your unrest and to more fully come to the source of all peace, Jesus.

The Source of Our Peace

1. (a) In Scripture, God is sometimes called "the God of peace" (Romans 15:33). Jesus is referred to as "the Lord of peace" (2 Thessalonians 3:16), and the prophet Isaiah, speaking about the coming Messiah, calls him the "Prince of Peace" (Isaiah 9:6). Peace has several dimensions: peace in our relationship with God; inner peace within our hearts and minds; and peace with our fellow human beings. Using the following passages, describe the foundation of our lasting peace.

Romans 5:1-2:

_____

_____

_____

Colossians 1:19-20:

_____

_____ ? _____

_____

_____

(b) How could the Sacrament of Reconciliation bring you more peace in your relationship with God?

_____

_____

_____

_____

> Earthly peace is the image and fruit of the _peace of Christ_, the messianic "Prince of Peace." By the blood of his Cross . . . he reconciled men with God and made his Church the sacrament of the unity of the human race and of its union with God. "He is our peace" (Ephesians 2:14).
>
> —*Catechism of the Catholic Church*, 2305

Inner Peace

2. What advice can you glean from the following passages that will help you to grasp and maintain the peace God provides?

Isaiah 26:3:

_____

_____

_____

_____

Philippians 4:6-7:

_____

_____

_____

_____

Philippians 4:8-9:

_____

_____

_____

_____

3. Peace is often disturbed by fear, either real or imagined. What are some typical circumstances where you find your inner peace frequently disturbed? Try to identify the cause of the apprehension as well as the circumstance.

_____

_____

_____

_____

Write a note to remind yourself of Jesus' promise: "Peace I leave with you; my peace I give to you" (John 14:27). Whenever you feel apprehensive, read this note.

Peace with Others

4. (a) In Romans 14:13-19, St. Paul was speaking about disagreements in the church between members who held to the Mosaic law and considered certain foods unclean and those who disregarded dietary restrictions. How does Paul urge church members to resolve the issue?

_____

_____

_____

(b) What does he say "makes for peace and for mutual upbuilding" (verse 19)?

_____

_____

_____

_____

(c) Is there a difficult situation you face, whether at work, at home, or in your parish, where you could "walk in love" (verse 15), as St. Paul advises, and bring peace and resolution?

_____

_____

_____

_____

Grant me, above all else, to rest in You, that my heart may find its peace in You alone; for You are the heart's true peace, its sole abiding place, and outside Yourself all is hard and restless. In this true peace that is in You, the sole, supreme, and eternal Good, I will dwell and take my rest. Amen.

—**Thomas à Kempis**, *The Imitation of Christ*

5. In what ways do you most need to grow in peace—in your relationship with God, in your relationship with others, or within your own heart and mind?

_____

_____

_____

_____

The Fruit of the Spirit Is Patience (Long-suffering)

Sometimes we encounter people who simply try our patience. And sometimes, rather than change the source of our vexation, the Spirit wants to transform us by changing us into longsuffering people. He does this because he wants us to better mirror God's love. Unfortunately, instead of patiently forbearing with others, we sometimes react with animosity and hostility. Having forgotten how patient God has been with us, we are tempted to return evil for evil and escalate the turmoil in our relationships.

Since we have the Holy Spirit dwelling in us, God has called us to reflect the mercy and grace we have experienced through Christ. He suffered for us so that we might realize that God loves us unconditionally and so that we might be healed. Similarly he often calls us to follow his example and endure the faults of others in a gracious manner so that they too might be healed as they realize that they are loved in spite of their sin. Of course, God never wants us to remain in situations in which we are being abused, physically or emotionally. But often, relating with our families or with those with whom we work simply requires us to exercise God's gift of patience and humility.

> **The Greek Translation**
>
> Generally speaking the word [*Makrothumia*] is not used of patience in regard to things or events but in regard to people. Chrysostom said that it is the grace of the man who could revenge himself and does not, the man who is slow to wrath.
> —**William Barclay**,
> *The Daily Bible Study Series*

God's Patience with Us

6. No one has had greater patience or long-suffering with us than God himself. Psalm 106 describes Israel's often erratic response to God, and God's immense patience with his people. By meditating on God's response to Israel, we can gain valuable insight as to what long-suffering truly means.

(a) Identify three or more ways in which God's people sinned against him and tested his love and patience.

_____

_____

_____

_____

(b) Although Israel provoked God's anger, how did God show long-suffering toward Israel?

_____

_____

_____

_____

(c) Share a situation in which God showed his patience with you.

_____

_____

_____

_____

There are some who remain at peace with themselves and also with others. And some neither have peace in themselves nor allow others to have peace. Such people are a trouble to others, and an even greater trouble to themselves. And there are some who are at peace with themselves, and who try to guide others into peace. But all our peace in this present life should depend on humble forbearance rather than on absence of adversity. He who knows the secret of endurance will enjoy the greatest peace. Such a one is conqueror of self, master of the world, a friend of Christ, and an heir of Heaven.

—**Thomas à Kempis**, *The Imitation of Christ*

Suffering Patiently Makes Us More like Jesus

7. Long-suffering involves how we respond to misbehavior and mistreatment that normally would warrant frustration, anger, or retribution. Reflect on 1 Peter 3:13-18, and then answer the following questions.

(a) According to these verses, how should we react when we are unfairly attacked?

_____

_____

_____

_____

(b) Why do you think Christ's sufferings are highlighted here (verse 18)?

_____

_____

_____

_____

(c) Why should we desire to have the fruit of long-suffering?

_____

_____

_____

_____

(d) Where in your life do you most often have occasion to be long-suffering?

_____

_____

_____

_____

Pray Together:

Lord, make me an instrument of your peace;
where there is hatred, let me sow love;
where there is injury, pardon;
where there is doubt, faith;
where there is despair, hope;
where there is darkness, light;
and where there is sadness, joy.

O Divine Master,
grant that I may not so much seek to be consoled as to console;
to be understood as to understand;
to be loved as to love;
for it is in giving that we receive,
it is in pardoning that we are pardoned,
and it is in dying that we are born to eternal life.

Peace Prayer of St. Francis of Assisi

▶ Preparing for Session 7

1. Each day, read some Scripture, perhaps meditating on one of the passages above that has touched you. Don't forget to record your thoughts in your prayer journal.

2. Complete the questions for the next session, "The Fruits of the Spirit Are Kindness and Goodness."

Notes for Session 6

Notes for Session 6

Session 7

The Fruits of the Spirit Are Kindness and Goodness

Take a few minutes to share insights with the other members in your Bible study from your prayer time and daily Scripture reading.

Kindness is the disposition we should have toward others. It is more than a feeling; it is a quality that causes us to *act* toward others in a kindly manner. Kindness and goodness are similar in nature, yet not identical. Goodness also involves a disposition of kindness toward others, but it includes an additional aspect of honesty or firmness in our relating with others that is meant to lead that person towards reform or change. In this session, we'll explore the following questions:

▶ **Why is the fruit of kindness more than just kind words?**

▶ **What are some ways in which the Lord has shown his kindness to us, and how does that help us to become more kind?**

▶ **How do we allow the Holy Spirit to put to death our flesh so that we can clothe ourselves with kindness?**

▶ **How did Jesus and St. Paul manifest the fruit of goodness?**

▶ **How can we grow so that the fruit of goodness flows to others?**

The Greek Translation

Kindness and goodness are closely connected words. For kindness the word is *chrestotes*. It, too, is commonly translated goodness. . . . The whole idea of the word is a goodness which is kind. The word Paul uses for goodness (*agathosune*) is a peculiarly Bible word and does not occur in secular Greek. . . It is the widest word for goodness; it is defined as "virtue equipped at every point." What is the difference? *Agathosune* might, and could, rebuke and discipline; *chrestotes* can only help. . . . The Christian needs that goodness which at one and the same time can be kind and strong.

—**William Barclay,**
The Daily Bible Study Series

Kindness . . . More than Words

Kindness is more than kind words—it flows to others through our actions. The Letter of James raises this question: "If a brother or sister is naked and lacks daily food, and one of you says to them, 'Go in peace, keep warm and eat your fill,' and yet you do not supply their bodily needs, what is the good of that?" (2:15-16). Hearing someone express pity toward another person who is in desperate straits, we might mistakenly conclude that he or she is being kind. But spiritual kindness must also compel us to act! Kindness, as a fruit of the Holy Spirit, should stimulate us to loving action toward others. A kind person recognizes that someone—a neighbor, friend, family member, or perhaps even a stranger—has a physical, mental, social, or spiritual need, and then helps to meet that need in some way.

1. (a) Kindness that results in action is described by Jesus in his parable of the Good Samaritan (Luke 10:30-37). What is the primary difference between the Samaritan and the others who saw the injured man?

   _____

   _____

   _____

   _____

   (b) What do you think causes seemingly good people not to act out of kindness?

   _____

   _____

   _____

   _____

Reflecting on God's Kindness toward Us

2. (a) We can perhaps best understand kindness by looking at the source of all aspects of godliness, the Lord himself. In Romans 2:1-5, why is judgment contrasted with kindness, and how does it help to define what kindness is?

_____

_____

_____

_____

(b) What is God's kindness meant to achieve, according to St. Paul?

_____

_____

_____

_____

(c) When you show kindness toward another, perhaps even someone who normally would warrant judgment, what effect can you expect your act of kindness to have?

_____

_____

_____

_____

"Putting on" the Clothing of Kindness

3. (a) Read Colossians 3:1-12. What do you think St. Paul meant when he urged the members of the early church to "strip off the old self with its practices" (verse 9)? Share some practical ways of doing this.

_____

_____

_____

(b) What do you think would happen if you simply tried putting on the clothes of kindness while the old self remained alive?

_____

_____

_____

_____

The Fruit of the Spirit Is Goodness

Here's an example of goodness: A doctor firmly lectures a couple in hopes of getting them to follow a medical regimen that will improve their health. The doctor could, uncaringly, simply prescribe some drugs and graciously ignore the real needs of the couple when they fail to follow the prescribed regimen. This, of course, would not be goodness. The spiritual fruit of goodness empowers us to speak with one another honestly and firmly. God loves each one of us, and asks us to love one another, even when it involves saying difficult things for that person's benefit.

When Jesus dealt firmly or sternly with others, it was not because he ran out of patience or abandoned his love for the people involved. Instead, Jesus spoke honestly with people as an act of kindness and love, and with the ultimate motive of doing good, both to them and to others who heard him. So let's begin by looking to see this quality in action in our Lord himself and in his apostle, St. Paul.

The Spiritual Fruit of Goodness in Jesus and St. Paul

4. On one occasion, Jesus admonished Martha, one of his closest friends. Read Luke 10:38-42. How does Jesus' answer to Martha demonstrate the quality of goodness?

_____

_____

_____

_____

5. Jesus was even sterner when he drove out the money changers in the Temple. Often we refer to Mark 11:15-18 as an illustration of Jesus' righteous anger. What made Jesus' cleansing of the Temple an act of goodness?

_____

_____

_____

_____

6. How do you see kindness accompanied with the healing quality of goodness in Jesus' response to the sinful woman in Luke 7:37-50?

_____

_____

_____

_____

7. Read Galatians 3:1-11. How does St. Paul also demonstrate the spiritual fruit of goodness in his dealings with the Christians in Galatia?

_____

_____

_____

_____

Growing in the Fruit of Goodness

8. How can you grow so that the fruit of goodness flows through your life to others more often?

_____

_____

_____

_____

9. What is the difference between simply expressing our annoyance with others and manifesting the character of goodness?

_____

_____

_____

_____

10. Why is it more effective for you to express kindness and goodness at the same time?

_____

_____

_____

_____

> In all truth one may claim: Tell me what moves you, and I will tell you who you are. God is moved by the suffering human heart; the pain of it clouds his face, and we understand who he is and what St. Paul means when he speaks of the 'goodness and kindness of God' (Titus 3:4). . . . He is the Lover who not only operates, but specifically acts in love.
>
> **—Romano Guardini**, *The Lord*

Pray Together:

Holy Spirit, God of light,
Fill us with your radiance bright;
Gentle father of the poor,
Make us, by your help, secure;
Come, your boundless grace impart
Bring your love to ev'ry heart.

Light immortal, fire divine,
With your love our hearts refine;
Come, our inmost being fill,
Make us all to do your will;
Goodness you alone can give
Grant that in your grace we live.

(Verses 1 and 3, *Veni Sancte Spiritus*, appearing in
The Liturgy of the Hours, Volume II)

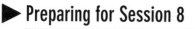 Preparing for Session 8

1. Each day, read some Scripture, perhaps meditating on one of the passages above that has touched you. Don't forget to record your thoughts in your prayer journal.

2. Complete the questions for the next session, "The Fruits of the Spirit Are Faithfulness, Meekness, and Temperance."

Notes for Session 7

Notes for Session 7

Session 8

The Fruits of the Spirit Are Faithfulness, Meekness, and Temperance

Take a few minutes to share insights with the other members in your Bible study from your prayer time and daily Scripture reading.

The three characteristics of the Spirit's fruit that we will be reflecting on in this session are faithfulness, meekness, and temperance—characteristics that all have to do with moderating our natural inclinations and replacing them with the quality of fortitude. In this session, we will seek to answer the following questions:

▶ **In what ways can Jesus be our source of faithfulness and move us to persevere faithfully as he did?**

▶ **How can we come to a clear understanding of how strong the meek person truly is?**

▶ **How can we learn real self-control, which is control of our passions?**

We Are Called to Be Faithful like Jesus

Faithfulness is that quality that enables a person to continue doing the right thing, even in the face of difficulty and obstacles. It stems from a deeply rooted confidence in God's truth and promises. Rooted and buttressed by this confidence, which is our faith, the faithful person remains committed to live and behave in a way consistent with the light that the Spirit has revealed to him or her.

The Greek Translation

Fidelity (*pistis*) is common in secular Greek for trustworthiness. It is the characteristic of the man who is reliable.

—**William Barclay,**
The Daily Bible Study Series

Someone has said that if you do the right thing for the wrong reason, you will eventually do the wrong thing. For instance, when encountering difficulties in an important relationship like that with a spouse, parent, or sibling, some people will give up on the relationship rather than trying to work things out. The virtue of faithfulness enables a person to continue doing the "right thing" (commitment to that relationship), for the right reason (out of love and because God is calling them to do so), even in the face of disappointment and difficulty. If our confidence is misplaced, then we will have a difficult time remaining faithful. When we are confident in God's promises, then we will find his strength to be faithful during seasons of trial.

Let's look at several passages regarding the value of the Spirit's fruit of faithfulness.

1. Faithfulness is tied to perseverance and trust in God. At his passion, Jesus was the supreme example of faithfulness, both to his Father and toward us. Read about Jesus' agony in the Garden (Luke 22:39-44). How was Jesus able to persevere?

   _____

   _____

   _____

   _____

2. According to Proverbs 25:19, how would you describe the characteristics of someone who is not faithful?

   _____

   _____

   _____

   _____

3. After reflecting on Luke 16:1-12, how can we prepare to be a faithful servant of Jesus, one who is entrusted with much for the Lord?

_____

_____

_____

_____

4. St. Joseph is an excellent example of someone who possessed the Spirit's fruit of faithfulness. Read Matthew 2:13-15, 19-23. What characteristics of faithfulness do you see in these incidents?

_____

_____

_____

_____

> Great opportunities to serve God rarely present themselves, but little ones are frequent. Whoever will be "faithful over a few things" will be placed "over many," says the Savior. "Do all things in the name of God," and you will do all things well.
> —**St. Francis de Sales**, *Introduction to the Devout Life*

Meekness Is Not Being Weak

Meekness may well be the most misunderstood characteristic of the Spirit's fruit. It is not a spirit of timidity or submissiveness, as people often think. Rather, meekness is possessed by confident, assured people who keep in check the power entrusted to them while remaining attuned and docile to the Spirit's leading.

Meekness is one of the two words Jesus used to describe himself in Matthew 11:29. If we have a misconception of what it means to be meek, this statement can be perplexing. How can the Son of God be meek if meekness is expressed by emotional timidity and submissiveness? How can the meek inherit the earth? In God's view, the one who should inherit the earth is not the person who allows his power to be ruled by misplaced emotions. Rather, it is the person who, like a powerful stallion controlled by the slightest touch of the rider's rein, submits his will to the rein—and reign—of the Spirit.

5. Read about Jesus' arrest and questioning before Pilate in John 19:1-11. In what ways did Jesus act meekly? Why?

_____

_____

_____

_____

_____

_____

_____

_____

The Greek Translation

In the New Testament [*praotes* for gentleness or meekness] has three main meanings. (a) It means being submissive to the will of God; (b) It means being teachable, being not too proud to learn; (c) Most often of all it means being considerate. . . . What throws most light on its meaning is that the adjective "praus" is used of an animal that has been tamed and brought under control; and so the word speaks of that self-control which Christ alone can give.
—**William Barclay**, *The Daily Bible Study Series*

6. Read Matthew 5:5. What promises are made to the person who is meek? Why do you think this is so?

_____

_____

_____

_____

7. Colossians 3:12-17 encourages us to clothe ourselves with meekness, compassion, kindness, humility, and patience. How does God want us to put on meekness and these other characteristics?

Temperance: Controlling Our Passions

In the late 1800s and early 1900s, the temperance movement was popular and growing in America. To combat the use of alcohol, temperance activists took for their motto a passage from Colossians: "Do not handle, Do not taste, Do not touch" (2:21). Ironically, when the passage is read in context, just the opposite concept is communicated. St. Paul was talking about human commands and teachings, which "have indeed an appearance of wisdom in promoting self-imposed piety, humility, and severe abasement of the body," but are "of no value in checking self-indulgence" (2:23). Temperance is not about a lifestyle of rules and regulations designed to imprison our tendency toward self-indulgence. Instead, temperance has to do with allowing the Spirit to produce within us strength of self-control, even when all external restraints have been removed.

The Greek Translation

Egkrateia [self-control or temperance] is the spirit which has mastered its desires and its love of pleasure. . . . It is the virtue which makes a man so master of himself that he is fit to be the servant of others.

—**William Barclay,**
The Daily Bible Study Series

Temperance is often translated as self-control, but perhaps its meaning would be communicated more accurately if we referred to it as passion-control. The person with temperance has been enabled by the Spirit to bring his passions under the control or rule of his renewed spirit, rather than to allow his passions to control his spirit. This ruling of our passions is impossible without the Holy Spirit's help to both conform our thinking to his will and to strengthen our will to do his bidding. See what you can discover about temperance in the following verses.

8. Read Proverbs 25:28. Why do we need the virtue of temperance?

_____

_____

_____

_____

9. According to 2 Timothy 1:6-7, who is the source of temperance, and how can we nurture this gift?

_____

_____

_____

_____

10. Read Galatians 5:16-17. How does the fruit of temperance relate to St. Paul's teaching on the desires of the flesh as opposed to the desires of the Spirit?

_____

_____

_____

_____

11. In what areas of your life would you like to exercise temperance more faithfully?

_____

_____

_____

_____

Pray Together:

> Breathe on [us], breath of God
> Fill [us] with life anew,
> That [we] may love the things you love,
> And do what you would do.
>
> Breathe on [us], breath of God,
> Until [our] hearts are pure,
> Until with you [we] have one will,
> To live and to endure.
>
> (Adapted from verses 1 and 2 of a hymn by Edwin Hatch, appearing in *The Liturgy of the Hours*, Volume II)

▶ Preparing for Session 9

1. Each day, read some Scripture, perhaps meditating on one of the passages above that has touched you. Don't forget to record your thoughts in your prayer journal.

2. Complete the questions for the next session, "The Gifts of the Holy Spirit."

Notes for Session 8

Notes for Session 8

Session 9

The Gifts of the Holy Spirit

Take a few minutes to share insights with the other members in your Bible study from your prayer time and daily Scripture reading.

The Holy Spirit is a gift to the church, proceeding from the Father and the Son, and in turn gives to the church all life and all gifts. The fulfillment of the promise in Acts 1:8, "You will receive power when the Holy Spirit has come upon you," is vividly seen throughout the Book of Acts. People are converted, healed, and resurrected. Jail doors are opened and prisoners set free. Individuals prophesy, speak in tongues, preach with power, and discern evil spirits. Men and women who one moment quake in fear behind locked doors in the next boldly lay down their lives as martyrs. Ordinary, uneducated men become successful in the cross-cultural spread of the gospel to vast areas and lay the foundations of a movement that has lasted nearly two thousand years.

These events are completely inexplicable apart from the supernatural power of the Holy Spirit. Rightly did Gamaliel predict, "If this plan or this undertaking is of human origin, it will fail; but if it is of God, you will not be able to overthrow them" (Acts 5:38-39). With the coming of the Holy Spirit, the work of God moved ahead in wisdom and power.

Come, Holy Spirit!

Such life, such power, is a desirable thing, but some, like Simon the magician, have coveted the power and gifts of the Holy Spirit for the wrong motives (Acts 8:9-24). We will do well to remind ourselves that we should seek the Giver and not just the gifts. The gifts of the Holy Spirit are wonderful, but the Giver surpasses the gifts and is the one we should desire and seek. When we are filled with him, we have access to all his gifts and graces, and he can distribute to us the gifts as we and the church have need.

So let us with one voice pray, "Come, Holy Spirit, fill us with your presence."

Let's look at the gifts the Holy Spirit distributes to the body of Christ. In this context, we will discover both his purposes in distributing these gifts and our responsibility to receive and exercise them in order to advance the kingdom of God and glorify Christ. Here are some questions we will explore in this session:

> ▶ **What are the gifts of the Spirit promised by God in the Old and New Testaments?**
> ▶ **How can we allow these gifts and virtues to rule our hearts?**
> ▶ **How can we pray to receive these gifts so that we build the body of Christ through them?**

A Variety of Gifts

1. The prophet Isaiah and the apostle Paul both spoke of the gifts of the Spirit. Isaiah's list refers to virtues which we all should possess, whereas Paul's list refers to charisms that are given individually and vary among different people.

Isaiah 11:1-2	1 Corinthians 12:4-10
Wisdom	Wisdom
Understanding	Knowledge
Counsel	Faith
Fortitude	Healing
Knowledge	Miracles
Piety	Prophecy
Fear of the Lord	Discernment of Spirits
	Tongues
	Interpretation of Tongues

What observations can you make about these lists? How are they similar and how are they different? In what ways have they been used to build up the church?

_____

_____

_____

_____

The Isaiah Gifts or Virtues

> The seven gifts of the Holy Spirit are wisdom, under-standing, counsel, fortitude, knowledge, piety, and fear of the Lord. They belong in their fullness to Christ, Son of David. They complete and perfect the virtue of those who receive them. They make the faithful docile in readily obeying divine inspiration.
>
> —*Catechism of the Catholic Church*, 1831

2. Isaiah 11:1-2 speaks of the seven gifts of the Spirit that would rest upon the Messiah and, through him, upon the church. According to Isaiah 11:3-5, how is the presence of these gifts of the Holy Spirit expressed through the Messiah?

_____

_____

_____

_____

The Catholic Encyclopedia describes how the gifts mentioned in Isaiah 11 can be expressed in your life:

- The gift of wisdom, by detaching us from the world, makes us relish and love only the things of heaven.
- The gift of understanding helps us to grasp the truths of religion as far as is necessary.

- The gift of counsel springs from supernatural prudence, and enables us to see and choose correctly what will help most to the glory of God and our own salvation.
- By the gift of fortitude we receive courage to overcome the obstacles and difficulties that arise in the practice of our religious duties.
- The gift of knowledge points out to us the path to follow and the dangers to avoid in order to reach heaven.
- The gift of piety, by inspiring us with a tender and filial confidence in God, makes us joyfully embrace all that pertains to His service.
- Lastly, the gift of fear fills us with a sovereign respect for God, and makes us dread, above all things, to offend Him.

3. (a) Which of these gifts would you like the Holy Spirit to enable you to experience more fully? Why? How would your life be different if you experienced these gifts?

_____

_____

_____

_____

(b) Do you believe the Holy Spirit will fill you with these gifts if you pray for them each day? How would your life be different if you prayed daily for these gifts?

_____

_____

_____

_____

The Corinthian or Charismatic Gifts

> Whether extraordinary or simple and humble, charisms
> are graces of the Holy Spirit which directly or indirectly
> benefit the Church, ordered as they are to the building
> up, to the good of men, and to the needs of the world.
> —*Catechism of the Catholic Church*, 799

4. (a) 1 Corinthians 12 contains the most comprehensive explanation of *charismata* gifts. According to verses 12:1, 7, 12-31, why does the Holy Spirit give us these types of gifts?

_____

_____

_____

_____

(b) People can respond to the gifts the Holy Spirit has given them, and to the gifts the Holy Spirit has given others, in several ways. According to St. Paul, what are the responses—both proper and improper—that are possible?

_____

_____

_____

_____

(c) Pick out one of the gifts, and describe what life would be like in the church if we all possessed that same gift and not any different gifts.

_____

_____

_____

_____

Gifts of Leadership

5. (a) Ephesians 4:11-16 lists gifts that seem to be in another category. What is the difference between these gifts and those in Isaiah and 1 Corinthians 12?

_____

_____

_____

_____

(b) Why do you think these gifts have been given to the church?

_____

_____

_____

_____

(c) What effect does the presence or absence of these gifts have on the members of Christ's body, the church?

_____

_____

_____

_____

Unity and Diversity

6. What is the connection between unity in the body of Christ and the diversity of gifts given to its members according to the following passages: Ephesians 4:1-6; 1 Corinthians 12:12-13, 20, 25; and Romans 12:4-5?

_____

_____

_____

_____

7. According to 1 Corinthians 12:31–13:3, what is the solution to not allowing our differing spiritual gifts to bring about disunity?

_____

_____

_____

_____

Praying for the Gifts

8. We see in Acts graphic examples of people filled with the Holy Spirit exercising their gifts in extraordinary ways. Read Acts 4:5-32; 8:4-8; and 9:10-18. After reflecting on these passages, write a personal prayer to the Holy Spirit expressing your desire to receive these gifts in your life.

_____

_____

_____

_____

Perhaps members of your group can pray with one another, asking the Holy Spirit in faith for the reception of these gifts.

Pray Together:

You are sevenfold in your gifts,
you are finger of God's right hand,
you, the Father's solemn promise
putting words upon our lips.

Grant we may know the Father through you,
and come to know the Son as well,
and may we always cling in faith
to you, the Spirit of them both.

(Stanzas 3 and 6 from *Veni Creator*, appearing in *Come, Creator Spirit* by Raniero Cantalamessa)

Congratulations! You have just completed *Living in the Power of the Holy Spirit Bible Study.* We hope and pray that you have found your life in Christ enriched and strengthened through your participation. No matter where you are in your journey of faith, know that God has more in store for you. Perhaps you and your group can take time to pray about what God wants you to do next in order to grow in your love of Jesus and your love of one another. May the Spirit of God fill you more deeply each day!

Acknowledgments (continued from page 3)

Quotations on pages 11 and 12 from *Meditation: The Bible Tells You How* by Jim Downing, Navpress, Colorado Springs, 1976.

Quotations on pages 22, 31, 63, 95, and 97 from the English translation of the *Catechism of the Catholic Church* for use in the United States of America, copyright © 1994, United States Catholic Conference, Inc., Libreria Editrice Vaticana. Used with permission.

Stanzas of *Veni Creator* on pages 26, 35, 46, 57, and 99 from *Come, Creator Spirit: Meditations on the Veni Creator* by Raniero Cantalmessa, translated by Denis and Marlene Barrett, The Liturgical Press, Collegeville, Minnesota, 2003.

Quotations on pages 30 and 40 from the Apostolic Exhortation *Christifideles Laici* (The Lay Members of Christ's Faithful People) by Pope John Paul II, issued December 30, 1988.

Quotations on pages 49, 53, 61, 66, 73, 83, 85, and 87 from *The Daily Bible Study Series, The Letters to the Galatians and Ephesians*, Revised Edition copyright © 1976, William Barclay, Westminster John Knox Press, Louisville, Kentucky.

Quotation on page 49 from *Interior Castle* by St. Teresa of Avila, translated and edited by E. Allison Peers, Image Books, New York, 1989.

Quotations on pages 51, 65, and 67 from *The Imitation of Christ* by Thomas à Kempis, translated by Leo Sherley-Price, Dorset Press, New York, 1986.

Quotation on page 52 from *In the Name of Jesus: Reflections on Christian Leadership* by Henri J. M. Nouwen, The Crossroad Publishing Co., New York, 1989.

Quotation on page 56 from *Fanny J. Crosby: An Autobiography,* Baker Book House, Grand Rapids, Michigan, 1999.

Quotation on page 78 from *The Lord,* by Romano Guardini, Regnery Publishing, Washington, D.C., 1996.

Quotation on page 79 from *Veni Sancte Spiritus,* ascribed to Stephen Langton (1150-1228), translated by Anthony G. Petti, appearing in *The Liturgy of the Hours,* Volume II, Catholic Book Publishing Co., New York, 1976.

Quotation on page 85 from *An Introduction to the Devout Life,* by St. Francis de Sales, translated by John K. Ryan, Image Books, New York, 1972.

Quotation on page 89 from a hymn by Edwin Hatch (1835-1889), adapted by Anthony G. Petti, appearing in *The Liturgy of the Hours,* Volume II, Catholic Book Publishing Co., New York, 1976.

Quotation on pages 95-96 from *The Catholic Encyclopedia,* Volume XIV, copyright © 1910 by Robert Appleton Company, Online Edition copyright © 2003 by K. Knight.

Notes

Notes

Notes

Notes

Notes

Notes

Notes

About the Author

Rich Cleveland and his wife Gail have been involved in ministry since 1974. Rich has served in several leadership positions at Holy Apostles Parish in Colorado Springs, Colorado, including as director of the Small Christian Communities Ministry for the past eight years. He and his wife have three grown children.

Rich also is director of Emmaus Journey: Catholic Small Group Ministry. Through this ministry, Rich and Gail have published several Scripture-based Catholic small group studies. Additionally, Rich publishes *Reflecting on Sunday's Readings*, a small group study based on each Sunday's Mass readings, which can be downloaded for free from the Emmaus Journey Web site at www.emmausjourney.org.

Rich has served as speaker and seminar leader at numerous national Christian conferences and conventions, including the Franciscan University of Steubenville's Men's Conference, the National Council of Catholic Evangelization, and St. Paul's Institute of Evangelical Catholic Ministry.

Also by Rich Cleveland

Learn from Scripture about the way of prayer, conversion, and faith from these Bible studies. The workbook-type format can help individuals seeking to understand Scripture, spouses who want to grow together in their faith, or Bible study groups.

Each Bible Study features:
- Solid Catholic understanding
- Questions for thought or discussion
- Important Scripture passages for each topic
- Plenty of room to write.

Serving the Master:
A Bible Study on Stewardship

Serving the Master reminds us of what it means to live out our baptismal vows as Catholics by truly being a eucharistic people. This Bible study explores the practical aspects of being good stewards of our hearts, lives, and mission.

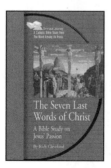

The Seven Last Words of Christ:
A Bible Study on Jesus' Passion

The Seven Last Words of Christ will help you to meditate and pray with Jesus as he endured the agony of the cross. Learn to pray with Jesus, "Father, forgive them . . ." and hear his comforting words, "Today, you will be with me in Paradise."

Stop by and see us as you journey on the Web

Emmaus Journey: Catholic Evangelization and Discipleship through Small Groups provides Scripture-based resources and foundational training in Catholic spirituality.

On the Emmaus Journey Web page, small group studies are *free* to download and reproduce for use in your parish. You will find additional small group resources and free downloads to assist you in your small group ministry.

In addition, at *The Word Among Us* Web page, we offer *free of charge*:
- the Scripture readings used at Mass for each day
- daily meditations and reflections based on the Mass readings
- practical articles on Christian living
- reviews of the newest Emmaus Journey Bible Studies.

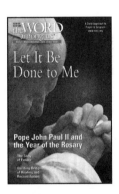

Please visit our Web sites today!

Emmaus Journey
www.emmausjourney.org
e-mail: info@emmausjourney.org
phone: 719-599-0448

www.wordamongus.org
e-mail: theresa@wau.org
phone: 800-775-9673